Us

50 Optical illusions

Written by Sam Taplin

Images by Hanri Van Wyk
and Matt Durber

Designed by Pete Taylor

Llyfrgelloedd Caerdydd
www.caerdydd.gov.uk/llyfrgelloedd
CAERDYDD Cardiff Libraries
CARDIFF www.cardiff.gov.uk/libraries

Did you notice that there's an
illusion on this page? You can find
out more about it on page 97.

ACC. No: 05078066

The world of illusions

Do you think you can trust your eyes? If so, this book is about to prove you very wrong. Over the next hundred pages you'll find a selection of bewildering optical illusions that will show you just how easily your eyes (and your brain) can be fooled. Here are just a few of the different types of illusions you'll be able to explore:

Brightness illusions

Take a look at the whale above. Its head is darker than its tail, right? Wrong! Actually the whole whale is exactly the same shade. There are many baffling "brightness" illusions like this, and you can find some more on pages 11, 57 and 101.

Slanting or straight?

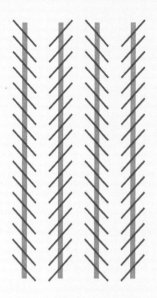

Stare at these lines for a moment. Do they look slanting? In fact, all the lines are absolutely straight and completely vertical. There are lots of ways to trick your eyes and make lines seem to bend – see pages 9, 55 and 65 for some more examples.

Shapes and sizes

Is the bottom shape bigger than the top one? Most people think so, but the two shapes are exactly the same size. Illusions based around shapes can be especially powerful – turn to pages 7, 15 and 33 to see some more.

How to use this book

Wherever you open this book, you'll find an optical illusion on the right-hand page. Once you've had a look at the illusion, you can turn the page to find out more about how it works.

For some of the illusions, you'll also have the chance to create your own version of the image by shading in or adding lines. Recreating an illusion yourself is a good way of understanding how it works.

To see lots more illusions and discover more about the vision science that makes them work, go to:

www.usborne.com/quicklinks

and type the keywords
50 optical illusions.

Please follow the internet safety rules displayed on the Usborne Quicklinks website.

Spinning circle

Stare into the middle of these circles and move your eyes left and right a little. What happens? Turn the page to find out more.

Spinning circle

When you stare at the circles, the inner one seems to rotate. This illusion depends on the fact that the arrows are white at the front and black at the back. You can see this more clearly in the enlarged arrows below. Although you might not notice this detail when you look at the circles, without it the illusion wouldn't happen.

Bewildering buildings

Look at the blue roof of each building. The two roofs seem to be very different in size and shape. But are they really? The next page will reveal the surprising truth.

Bewildering buildings

Incredibly, the two roofs are exactly the same size and shape. This is so hard to believe that you'll need to measure the shapes to prove it.

One reason this illusion is so powerful is that we can see that one of the buildings is long and thin, while the other is square. Therefore our brains are telling us that the tops of the buildings must be very different. Try drawing your own buildings beneath the shapes below – do the shapes look more different now?

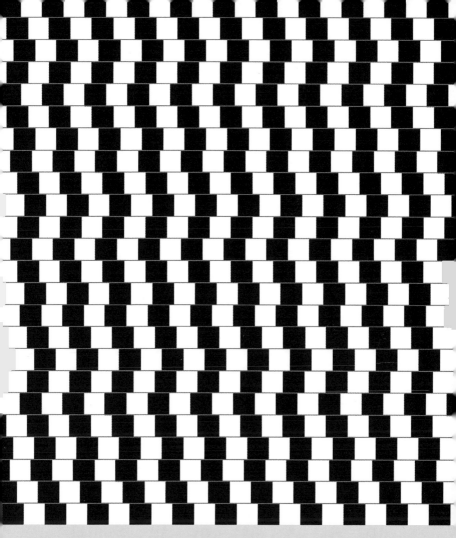

The café wall illusion

Are the horizontal lines across this image slanting? Or are they parallel? Take a good look, then turn the page.

The café wall illusion

All the horizontal lines are parallel, but the arrangement of black and white bricks makes it almost impossible to see this. This is called the "café wall" illusion. It was first discovered when someone noticed that the pattern on a café wall had accidentally created this very powerful effect.

You can create your own version of the illusion with the image below. Just shade all the dotted bricks black, and you'll see how the lines seem to become slanted.

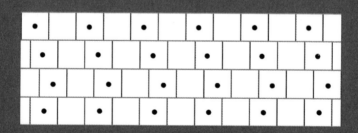

Wacky waves

Look at the wave that each surfer is riding.
They seem to be very different shades. But
are they really? Turn the page to find out.

Wacky waves

Amazingly, both waves are exactly the same shade. The other waves that surround them alter the way that we see them, making the top one seem pale and the bottom one much darker. You can see how this works below – the wave across the middle is all the same shade, but it doesn't appear to be.

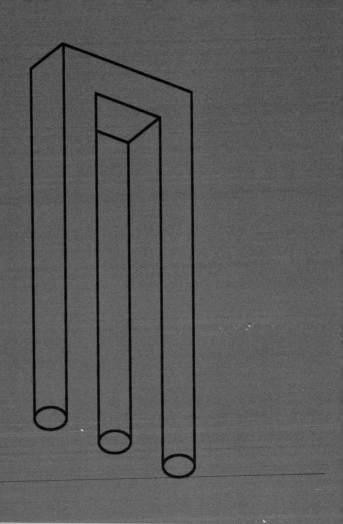

Impossible fork

How many prongs does this fork shape have?
Look at the end of the middle one, then follow
it back. What happens?

Impossible fork

The fork illusion is one of the most famous "impossible objects" – shapes that seem normal when you first look at them, but would actually be impossible to build. The fork has both two prongs, and three!

There are lots of these objects. You can see another one below – an impossible staircase. The bottom of the staircase, at the bottom left, is on the same level as the top of the staircase at the top right.

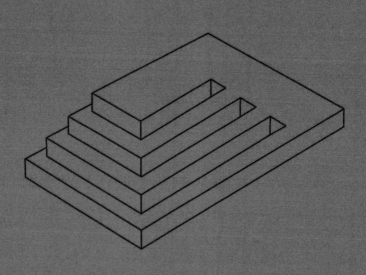

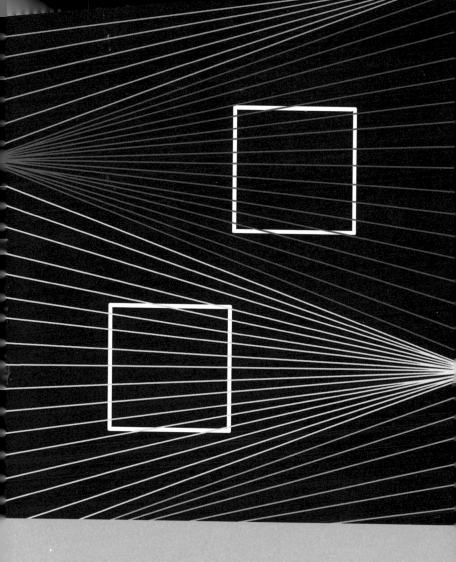

Squashed squares

Are the white squares distorted? Or are they perfect squares? Take a good look, then turn the page.

Squashed squares

The squares are perfectly regular, but the pattern of lines makes it look as if they're bending out of shape. You can create the same effect with the square below. Use a ruler to draw straight lines from the dot on the left to each dot on the right. How does the square look now?

Shaking star

Look at the star shape in the middle of
this image, then shake the book gently
left and right. What happens?

Shaking star

When you move the image around, the star shape seems to shake and wobble against the background. This illusion relies on the fact that the star and the background have the same pattern, but at different angles. The blurred background makes the illusion even stronger. If you remove the background pattern, the star won't move if you shake the book, as you can see below.

Spooky spider

Get a blank piece of paper, then stare at the red dot above for at least 30 seconds, trying not to blink. Now stare at the blank paper. What do you see?

Spooky spider

When you stare at the paper you should see a black spider. This kind of illusion is called an after effect. The same thing happens when you stare at any image for a long time – try drawing your own simple picture in the space below and see if you can make the same kind of illusion work.

Tilting rectangles

Are the rectangles in this image slanting? Or are they perfect rectangles? Turn the page to find out more.

Tilting rectangles

The rectangles aren't slanting at all – the sides are straight and they all line up with each other. But the pattern of lines in the background creates a strong illusion that the rectangles are tilting in different directions. Part of the pattern has been removed in the image below, so you can see how the illusion vanishes in that section.

Whirlpool fooler

Move your eyes around this whirlpool.
Are you looking at one continuous
spiral? Or is it lots of separate circles?
You can find out on the next page.

Whirlpool fooler

The whirlpool is made up of lots of separate circles – there's no spiral in the image at all. But the way the image is drawn makes it hard to see this, as your eyes tend to be sucked inwards by the pattern.

Below you can see the same image with one of the circles highlighted in black. Now it's easier to see that there's no spiral.

Topsy-turvy faces

Look at the monster at the bottom. Now, without turning the book upside down, look at the other one. Do you see anything strange? Turn the page to find out what's happening.

Topsy-turvy faces

When you turn the book around and look at the top monster the other way up you'll find it has a very strange face – its mouth, nose, eyes and ears are upside down! But until you turn the image around this is quite hard to spot. Our brains tend to "correct" the image because we know how a face normally looks. See if you can draw your own version of this illusion by adding details to the faces below.

Dizzy grid

Have a good look at this grid. The lines seem to be wobbly, don't they? Or are they straight? Look at the next page to find out.

Dizzy grid

Every single line in the grid is absolutely straight. But the pattern of little squares inside the larger ones makes it very hard for our eyes to see this.

If you look at the same grid with some of the little squares removed it's easier to view it clearly, as you can see below.

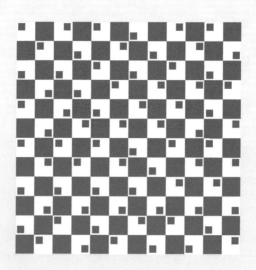

Dancing dots

Move your eyes around the black lines in this image. Do you see anything strange? The next page will explain what's going on.

Dancing dots

When you move your eyes around the image, you should see little pale dots appearing and disappearing on the black lines at the corners of the triangles. If you stare at any one dot it will vanish, but you'll keep seeing them out of the corners of your eyes.

Use a black pen to fill in the lines of the grid below – can you make the illusion happen?

Curious cat

Is this cat facing you, or does it have its back
to you? Can you see it both ways? Can you add
lines to make it look at you, or away from you?
The next page will show you how.

Curious cat

The cat could be facing you or looking away
from you – it's impossible to say which, and
your eyes will keep "flipping" between the
two ways of seeing it. See below for how
you can add just a few lines to make the
silhouette into two different images.

Can you draw another animal silhouette that
can be viewed in two different ways like this?

Strange circles

Are the circles on the right squashed?
Or are they perfect circles? Take a good
look before you turn the page.

Strange circles

The circles are all perfectly round. But the pattern of lines drawn onto each one confuses our eyes and makes the circles seem squashed out of shape.

As you can see below, the same kind of illusion can be created with squares. It's hard to believe that the sides of these two squares are all straight... but they are!

Stars and stripes

Look at the red stripes on these two
stars. Are they different shades of red?
The next page will tell you.

Stars and stripes

The red stripes on both stars are exactly the same shade, but the other stripes change the way we see them: the red in the top star looks almost purple, while the same red in the bottom one seems more like orange. In fact, if you look at the illusion from a distance you won't see stripes at all – the red will blend with the other shades and you'll just see a purple star and an orange one, like the ones below.

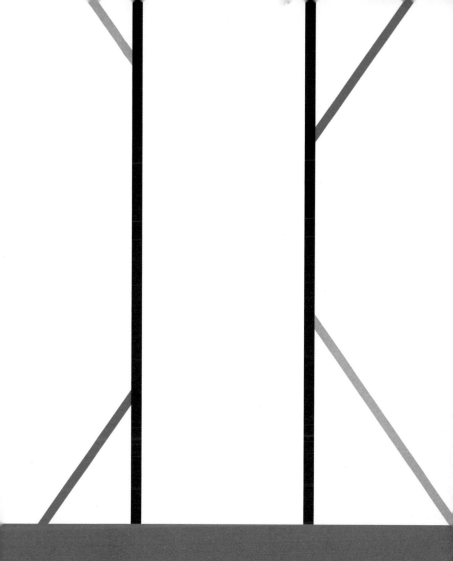

Broken lines?

Look at the red stripes. Do they line up with each other? How about the blue ones? Turn the page for the answer.

Broken lines?

The two red stripes line up perfectly – they're part of the same line. The blue ones are also part of the same line. You can prove this is true by using a ruler to check. This strange illusion always happens when you draw a straight line and then remove the middle section. Try drawing a line below and then covering up the middle part – do the end sections look as if they no longer line up?

Vanishing vase

When you first look at this image you'll probably see a yellow vase. But if you focus on the blue part of the picture instead, you'll see something quite different. What is it?

Vanishing vase

This illusion is one of the most famous examples of an "ambiguous image" – an image which can be seen in two totally different ways. It all depends on which part of the picture you think of as the foreground. If you think the middle part is the foreground, then it's a vase. But if you think of that part as the background, then you see two faces. If you move the faces further apart, the vase starts to vanish, as you can see below.

Who's there?

Shake this image gently left and right, or look at it from far away. Do you see anything hiding among the stripes? Turn the page to find out who's there.

Who's there?

There's an alien hiding among the stripes! This is very hard to see, but when you shake the page it flickers into view.

This illusion works because only very thin strips of the alien are present on the page. When the image isn't moving, these strips blend into the pattern. But when you move the image, your brain connects up all the little strips to "make" the alien. So you're seeing something that isn't quite there.

Focus pocus

Do parts of this image seem to be out of focus? Do those parts look "further away" than the clear parts? Look at the next page for more about this illusion.

Focus pocus

Because of the way this image is drawn,
it's almost impossible not to see the square
sections as out of focus and far away.

If you try to see the image as just one flat
surface, without foreground or background,
you'll find it's not easy.

Without the blurring on the square sections,
the illusion disappears, as you can see below.

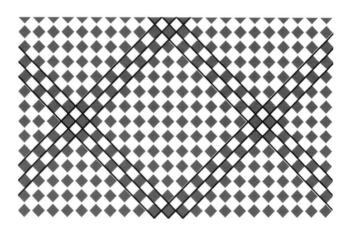

Long and short?

Look at these two horizontal lines. Is the top one longer than the bottom one? Turn the page to find out.

Long and short?

The two lines are exactly the same length. The only reason we see them differently is the circles that have been added to each end.

This famous illusion is a classic example of how easy it is to make identical lines look different. Try adding circles to the ends of the lines below, copying the positions of the ones on the last page – can you make one line look longer than the other?

Parallel puzzler

Move your eyes around this grid.
Are the lines slanting? Or are they parallel?
The next page will tell you.

Parallel puzzler

The grid is entirely regular – all the white lines are straight and parallel. But the pattern of diagonal lines confuses our brains and makes it hard to see this.

In the image below, half of the pattern has been removed. Can you see how this affects the illusion? The vertical lines look parallel, but the horizontal ones still seem to slant.

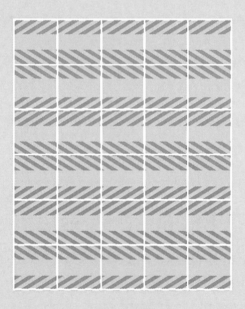

Shining shape

Look at the middle section of this image. Is it a different shade of blue from the background? Does it look brighter? Once you've had a look, turn the page.

Shining shape

The middle of the shape is exactly the same shade of blue as the background. But the blurred edges of the middle section change the way we see the whole thing. If you want to prove this, carefully draw a sharp black edge around the middle of the shape below. You'll then be able to see that it's the same shade as the background.

Spinning circles

Move your eyes around this image.
Do the circles seem to be spinning around?
What happens if you stare at one circle?

Spinning circles

This illusion is more effective when there are several circles, because the circles spin far more when you're not looking directly at them. Notice, for example, what happens to the circles at the bottom of this page while you're reading this sentence – are they moving? Now stare directly at one of the circles, and you'll find it stops!

Fishy problem

Look at the wide vertical stripes made by the fish scales in this pattern. Are the stripes tilting? Or are they parallel? The next page will tell you.

Fishy problem

It's hard to believe, but the stripes are totally parallel. No one is quite sure how this illusion works, but it's created by the complex pattern around the stripes. Every part of the pattern is needed to create the illusion, as you can see below: if you look at the same image with the background removed, the illusion works slightly less well.

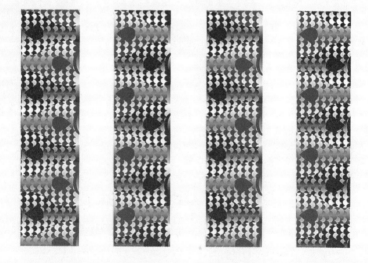

Bulging squares

Are the thin lines in this grid of squares curved? Or are they completely straight? Take a good look, then turn the page.

Bulging squares

All of the lines in the grid are completely straight, but it's hard to see them that way. The pattern on the grid creates a strong illusion that the lines are bending away from the middle, and makes it hard for our brains to see the lines as they really are.

The bottom of the image below has part of the pattern removed. Without those extra lines the illusion vanishes, as you can see.

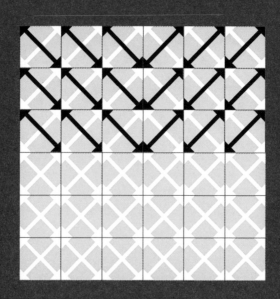

Confusing chameleons

The spots on these two chameleons seem
to be different shades of blue. But are they
really so different? The next page will
reveal the truth.

Confusing chameleons

The spots on both chameleons are exactly the same shade of blue, but the contrasting backgrounds make it very hard to see this. To most people, the spots on the top chameleon look darker than the bottom one.

Below you can see a simpler version of this very powerful illusion – both blue circles are the same. You can prove this by covering up everything except the circles.

Spooky visitor

Stare at this image and move the book left and right. Can you see something spooky appearing at the window?

Spooky visitor

When you move the image, or look at it from far away, you should see a ghost appearing at the window.

This illusion works because only very thin strips of the ghost are drawn on the page. When the image isn't moving, these strips get lost in the pattern, but when you move the image your brain connects up all the little strips to "make" the ghost. See page 41 for a similar illusion.

Square sizes

Take a quick look at the two blue squares in this image. Are they different sizes? Turn the page to find out.

Square sizes

The two blue squares are exactly the same size, but the red squares around them make it hard to see them that way.

Can you draw more squares onto the image below to create the same sort of effect?

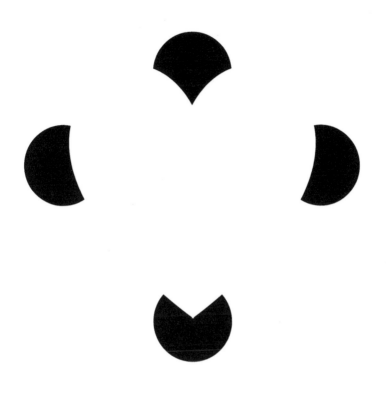

Ghostly shape

Can you see a white shape in this image? Does it look brighter than the white background? Is it really there? The next page will tell you.

Ghostly shape

The image seems to have a white heart in
the middle of it. But in fact there's nothing
there at all – we just assume there must
be a heart because of the gaps in the little
circles around the edges. The illusion is so
convincing that we "see" the whole shape
and it seems to stand out slightly against
the background. Below you can see another
illusion that uses the same principle – what
shape do you see in this one?

Leaning lamp posts

Are these lamp posts tilting away from each other? Or are they parallel? Look carefully at them, then turn the page.

Leaning lamp posts

The lamp posts are parallel, and this is completely obvious if you remove the rest of the image, as you can see below. All that's needed to create the illusion are the little diagonal stripes going in a different direction on each post. If you carefully copy the stripes onto the posts below, you'll see them appear to tilt in the same way.

Triangle teaser

In the triangle there's a black X, a white X and a blue X. Which one do you think is exactly halfway up the triangle? Decide on your answer, then turn the page.

Triangle teaser

Surprisingly, the blue X is halfway up the triangle. Most people think it's the white one, or even the black one. This simple effect is quite deceptive, and it's easy to create your own version. Try adding a dot exactly halfway up the triangle below, using a ruler to measure. Now remove the ruler and look at the dot – it probably seems higher than halfway!

Dark and pale

This image seems to have pale yellow sections and darker yellow sections. But does it really? Take a look, then turn the page.

Dark and pale

The whole image is exactly the same shade of yellow, but the black lines make the yellow seem darker and the white lines make it seem paler. This is because our brains "mix" the black or white into the yellow slightly.

The image below is all the same shade of yellow, even though the left half looks darker. If you carefully trace over the white lines in black, you can make the illusion disappear.

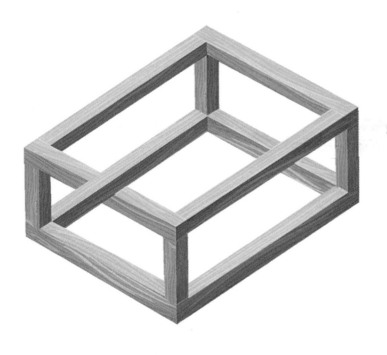

Impossible crate

This crate looks normal at first. But is it? Would it be possible to build it? You can find out on the next page.

Impossible crate

If you tried to build the crate, you wouldn't be able to. It's a famous example of an "impossible object" – something that looks normal at first but actually makes no sense and couldn't exist in the real world. Below you can see another classic one – a triangle that might seem logical at first, but becomes weirder and weirder the more you look at it.

Vertical lines?

Are the vertical lines in this image slanting away from the middle? Or are they parallel? Turn the page to find out the truth.

Vertical lines?

The lines are completely parallel and vertical, but the blurred pattern behind them makes it very hard for us to see this. In the image below, some of the pattern has been removed – now it's easier to see that the red lines aren't actually slanting at all.

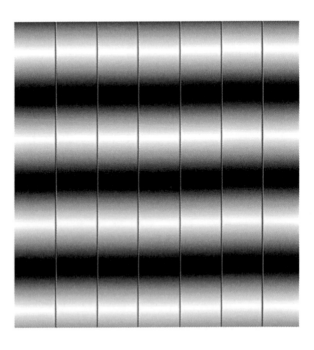

Out of focus

Is the square on the left darker than the one on the right? Take a good look, then turn the page.

Out of focus

Both squares are exactly the same shade, and the only difference is the blurred outline of the right-hand square. This confuses our eyes and makes us think that the entire square must be slightly fuzzy and pale compared to the other one.

Use some strips of paper to cover up the fuzzy edges on the right-hand square below. Does the illusion vanish when the blurred edges are hidden?

Wobbly squares

Stare at the middle of this image, and
move the book slowly up and down.
What happens?

Wobbly squares

When you move the book, there's a powerful illusion of movement – the middle column of squares seems to wobble left and right. This happens because the squares have some black edges and some white ones. If you make all the edges the same, the illusion vanishes, as you can see below: if you move this page up and down you won't see any movement in the all-white squares.

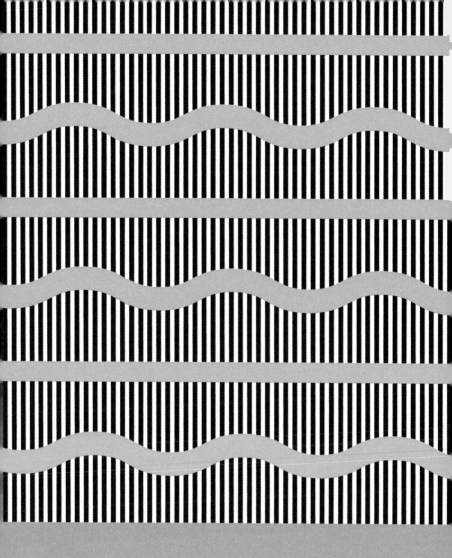

Shimmers and glimmers

Look at the blue lines in this image.
Do they seem to shimmer and flash with
little white dots and streaks?

Shimmers and glimmers

This illusion happens because of the black and white stripes in the background. When we look at solid blue surrounded by these stripes, we see flashes of white, or tiny white dots, going up and down.

It's useful to compare how it looks if you remove the black and white background: you shouldn't see any shimmers of white on the blue stripes below. Now look back at the ones on the last page – quite a difference...

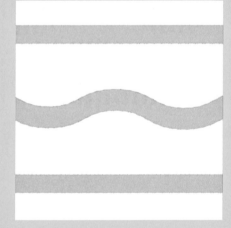

How long?

Is one of the blue lines longer than the other? Take a quick look, then turn the page to find out.

How long?

Both blue lines are the same length. But the pattern of other lines creates the illusion that the one on the right is slightly longer. This is because the line on the left is surrounded by long lines, making it seem shorter, while the line on the right has shorter lines around it, which make it seem longer. As you can see below, if all the other lines are the same length then the illusion disappears.

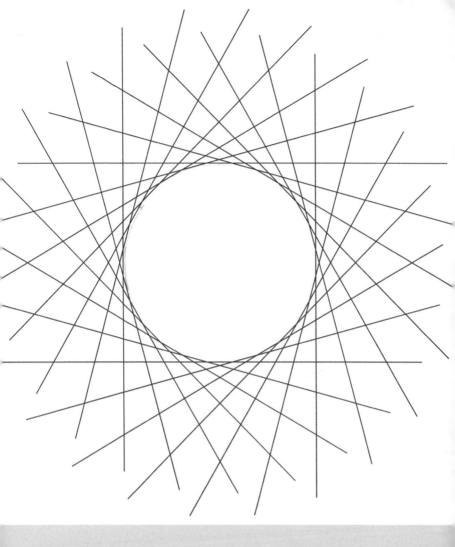

Straight circle

Look at the circle in the middle of this image.
Can you see anything strange about it? Does
it actually exist? The next page will tell you.

Straight circle

The image has no curved lines in it. The "circle" is made up of lots of straight lines at different angles. You can see how this works and create your own "curve" in the box below. Just use a ruler to join up each pair of dots that are the same shade, and you'll see the curve start to take shape.

Surprising spots

The giraffe on the left has dark orange spots,
and the one on the right has pale orange spots.
But are the two oranges really different?
You can find out on the next page.

Surprising spots

Amazingly, the spots on both giraffes are the same shade of orange. The reason they look so different is that our brains are tricked by the backgrounds: the spots on the right look pale against a dark background, while the ones on the left are against a much paler background so they appear darker.

Notice how the illusion remains even when you add a solid orange bar to the picture: instead of making the spots look the same, the bar actually seems to change as you look from left to right!

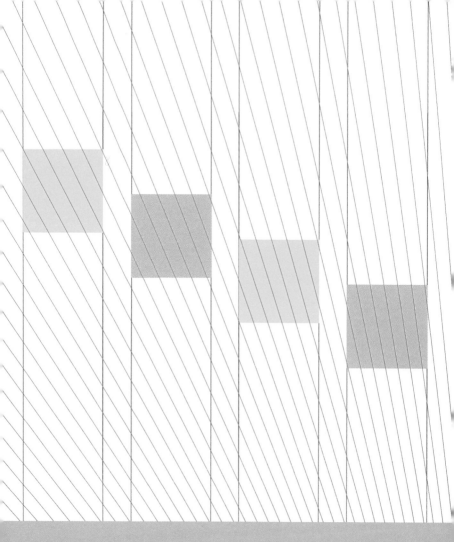

Tilting squares

Are these squares wonky or are they perfect squares? Do the red lines tilt to the right or are they straight? You'll find the answer to both questions on the next page.

Tilting squares

All of the shapes are perfect squares, and all the red lines go straight up the page – they don't tilt at all. Surprisingly, all it takes to bring about these two strong illusions is the pattern of slanting lines in the background.

Can you add lines to the image below to create the same illusion? Look at the picture on the last page and use a ruler to draw your lines at the same kind of angle.

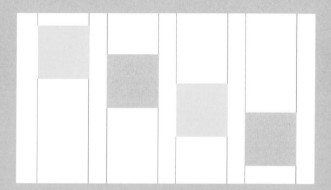

Fading dots

Keep your eyes fixed on the dot in the middle of this image for at least 30 seconds. What happens to the other dots?

Fading dots

When you stare at the middle of the image, the dots around the edges should slowly fade, and even disappear completely. In fact, if you stare for long enough, even the dot in the middle may vanish. This effect is much more powerful because the dots are fuzzy and blurred – if you try the same thing with dots that are sharp and clear, like the ones below, they won't fade as easily.

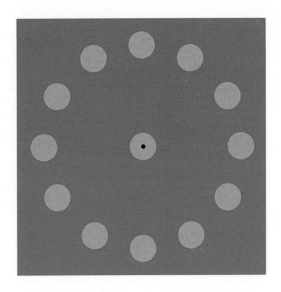

Swirling shapes

Stare at the middle of this image and
move the book around. What do you see?
Turn the page to find out more.

Swirling shapes

When you move the image around, you should see ghostly shapes flickering around the middle, like the one drawn onto the image below. No one is quite sure why the black and white lines cause this strange illusion to happen.

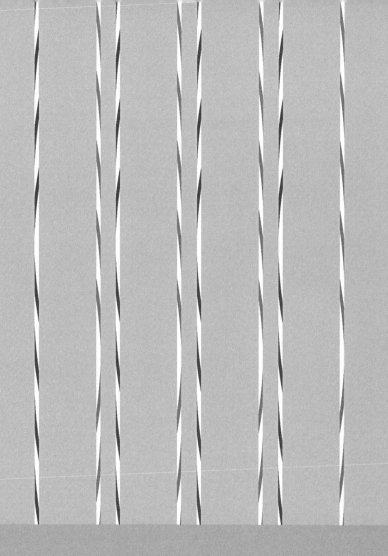

Curved lines?

All these lines look as though they curve a little. But do they really? Take a look, then turn the page to find out.

Curved lines?

All of the lines are straight and parallel,
but this is very hard to see because of the
patterns on the lines.

If you remove the patterns from some lines
it's clear that all the lines are straight, as you
can see below.

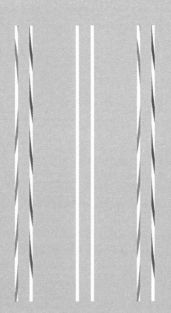

All the same?

Look at the rectangles inside these frames. They all seem to be more or less the same. But are they really? The next page will tell you.

All the same?

Although the rectangles all look very similar, they are in fact all different, as you can see below. The bright frame around each rectangle changes the way we see it, so that blue and purple and green and brown can all be made to look a very similar shade.

Rocky rows

At first glance it seems obvious that these rows of circles are tilting. But are you sure they are? Turn the page for the answer.

Rocky rows

The rows of circles aren't tilting at all, but the pattern of lines on top of them creates the illusion that they're slanting. If you remove those lines the illusion is less effective, as you can see below. For another amazing version of this illusion, look back at the first page of this book – believe it or not, the circles form a perfect rectangle!

Ghostly grid

Can you see lots of little white circles in this image? Do they seem brighter than the white background? Do they join up to form a grid?

Ghostly grid

There are no little circles in the image, but the gaps in the lines make it almost impossible not to see them. You can create the same effect by covering parts of the lines below with a black pen. Just draw a black cross over each yellow one.

If you look back at the last page you'll find it's also possible to see squares in the gaps, rather than circles. If you tell yourself that they are squares, that's what you'll see!

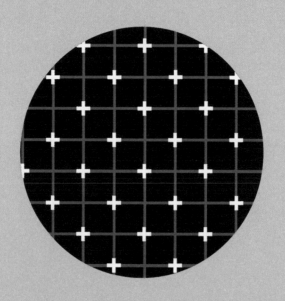

Chessboard challenge

The two circled squares seem very different – one looks dark and the other pale. But are they as different as they appear? Look at them carefully, then turn the page.

Chessboard challenge

Amazingly, the two squares are exactly the same shade. This extraordinary effect is created by the shadow across the right-hand side of the image. We see the right-hand square as a pale one with a shadow across it, rather than what it really is – a dark square. In the image below, a stripe has been added which is the same shade as both squares. But the illusion remains – it looks as though the stripe changes as you go from left to right.

Deceptive lines

It looks as though the line going up this page is longer than the one along the bottom. But is this really true? The next page will reveal all.

Deceptive lines

Although the image on the last page is very simple, it's also a remarkably powerful illusion: both lines are the same length. The illusion relies partly on the fact that we always tend to overestimate the length of vertical lines and underestimate the length of horizontal ones. The extra lines added to the image on the front of this page make the illusion more effective. Copy the same lines onto the image below to make it stronger.

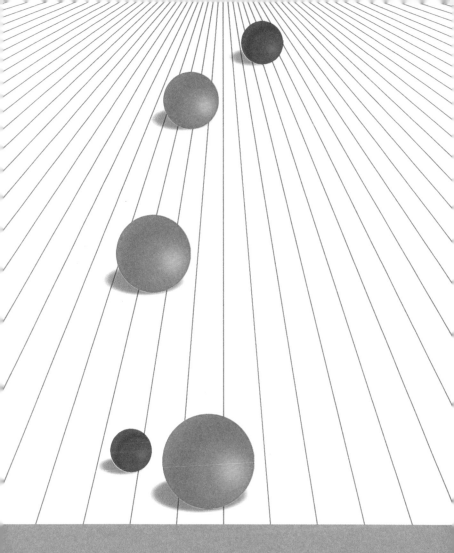

In the distance

Look at the two red balls. Is the one at the top slightly bigger than the one at the bottom? Turn the page to find out.

In the distance

The two red balls are exactly the same size. The reason we tend to see the one at the top as bigger is that it's far away from us in the picture. Therefore we interpret that ball as a very big ball which is far away, and the other one as a little ball which is close up.

Try cutting out a small shape and then drawing around it at the top and bottom of the image below. Do your two identical shapes seem to be different sizes?

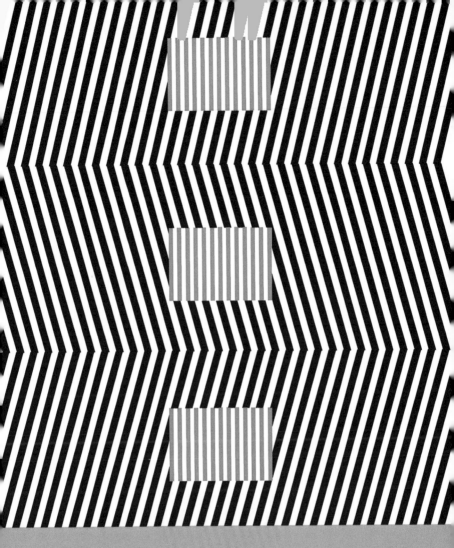

Baffling blocks

Look at the blocks of orange and white stripes. Do those stripes all line up, or is the block in the middle tilting to the right? The next page will tell you.

Baffling blocks

All the orange and white stripes are totally parallel, but the tilting stripes behind them create the illusion that they're slightly slanted.

Below you can see a simpler version of this illusion – the two blocks seem to be tilting slightly in different directions. If you cover up the rest of the image, you'll find it easier to see that the stripes in the two blocks line up perfectly.

Cube conundrum

Look at these cubes. Can you see
which way up they are? Are you sure?
Keep looking for a while before you
turn the page.

Cube conundrum

There are two different ways of viewing the image on the last page. Each side of each cube could also be the side of a different cube – it depends how you look at it, and your eyes will keep "flipping" between different ways of seeing the cubes. The top shape below has two different cubes in it, and the cubes at the bottom show the different ways of seeing it.

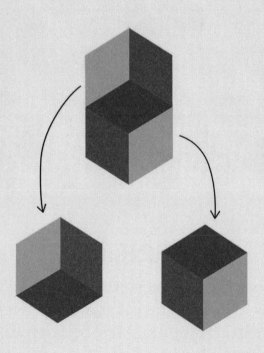

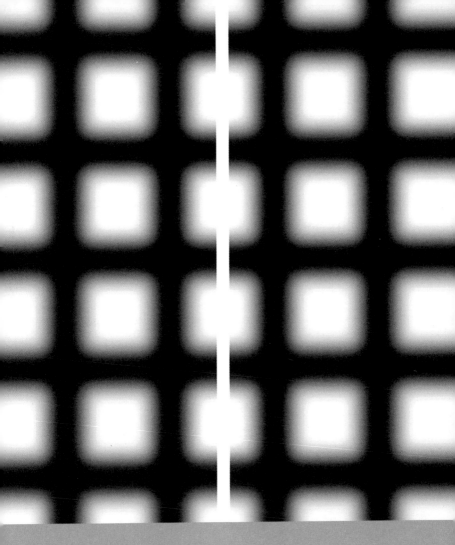

Light and shade?

Look at the white stripe in the middle.
Are some parts of it brighter than
others? Turn the page to find out.

Light and shade?

The whole stripe is exactly the same shade. But the image behind it makes it look as though some sections are darker than others. Try covering up the whole image below apart from the white stripe – it should now be clear that the stripe is all the same. Then reveal the whole image again, and the stripe will seem to change.

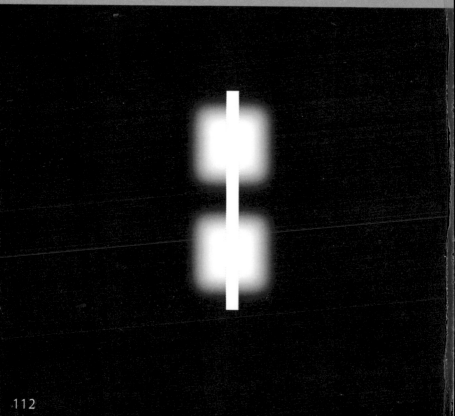